octopuses

BY KARA L. LAUGHLIN

The Child's World®
childsworld.com

Published by The Child's World®
1980 Lookout Drive • Mankato, MN 56003-1705
800-599-READ • www.childsworld.com

DESIGN ELEMENTS
© creatOR76/Shutterstock.com: porthole
© keren-seg/Shutterstock.com: water

PHOTO CREDITS
© Boris Pamikov/Shutterstock.com: 9; David Evison/Shutterstock.com: 12-13; George P. Gross/Shutterstock.com: 14; Jeff Rotman/NPL/Minden Pictures: 11; LauraD/Shutterstock.com: 15, 17, 20-21; Richard Whitcombe/Shutterstock.com: 5; Vittorio Bruno/Shutterstock.com: 6-7, 8, 18-19; Vladimir Wrangel/Shutterstock.com: cover, 1

ISBN: 9781503816879
LCCN: 2016945606

Printed in the United States of America
PA02326

NOTE FOR PARENTS AND TEACHERS

The Child's World® helps early readers develop their informational-reading skills by providing easy-to-read books that fascinate them and hold their interest. Encourage new readers by following these simple ideas:

BEFORE READING

- Page briefly through the book. Discuss the photos. What does the reader think he or she will learn in this book? Let the child ask questions.
- Look at the glossary together. Discuss the words.

READ THE BOOK

- Now read the book together, or let the child read the book independently.

AFTER READING

- Urge the child to think more. Ask questions such as, "What things are different among the animals shown in this book?"

Contents

Hiding in the Sea

An animal is hiding in the sea. Can you find it? It is an octopus.

Octopuses live all over the world. Some live near land. Some live in deep water.

Did you know?

There are about 300 species of octopuses.

Eight Arms

An octopus has two eyes. It has a rounded head area called a **mantle**. Most important, an octopus has eight arms.

Did you know?

Some octopuses can be up to 16 feet (5 meters) long from arm tip to arm tip.

An octopus's arms have suckers.
The suckers grip, taste, and feel.

Did you know?

Each arm has two rows of suckers.

The suckers help the octopus move.
They also help it to hunt.

Eating

Octopuses eat crabs, shrimp, and shellfish. An octopus has a strong **beak**. It is in the middle of the octopus. It can bite through shells.

Did you know?

An octopus's beak is made of the same stuff as your fingernails.

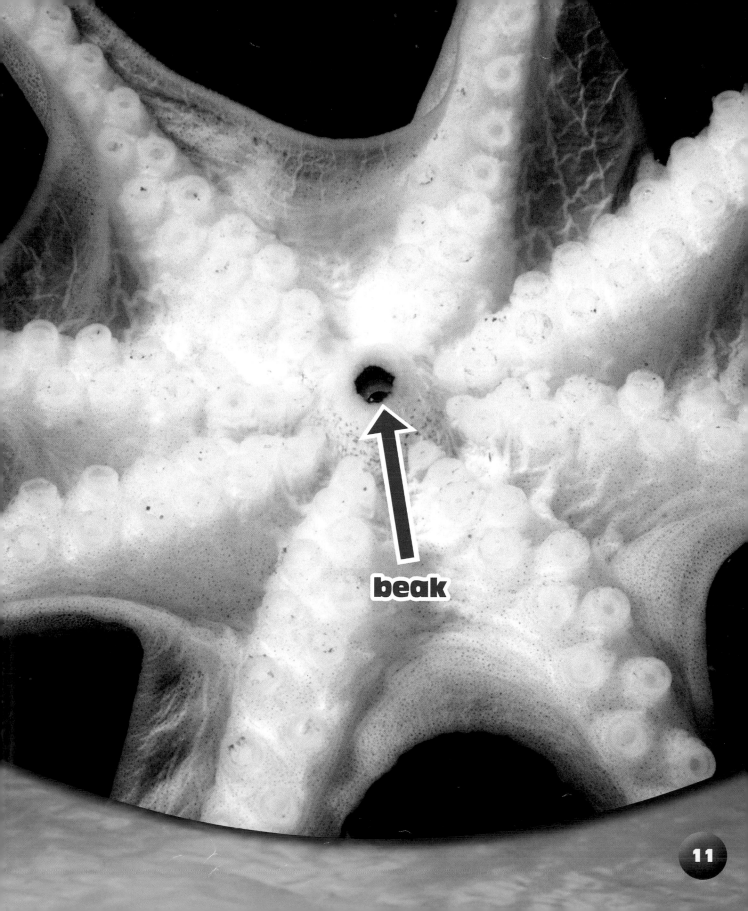

beak

No Bones

An octopus has no bones. It is squishy. That means it can get through tiny holes. An octopus can go anywhere its beak can fit.

Did you know?

An octopus has 3 hearts.

Good Hiders

Octopuses like to hide. They spend most of their day in a **den**.

Did you know?

An octopus can change color in less than a second.

Octopuses can change the color of their skin. Their skin can change shape, too. This helps them blend in.

Baby Octopuses

After mating, a female octopus goes to her den. She lays thousands of tiny eggs. She guards them and keeps them clean. Soon the eggs hatch. The tiny baby octopuses float away.

Did you know?

Octopus eggs are about the size of a grain of rice.

Did you know?

An octopus can swim up to 25 miles (40 kilometers) per hour.

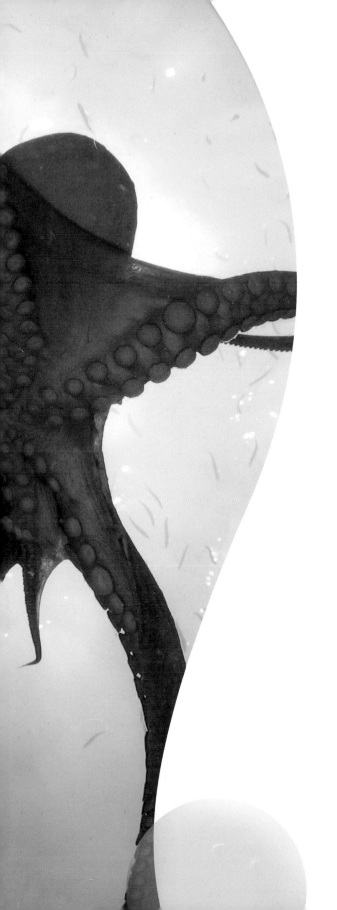

Inky Getaway

Many sea animals like to eat octopuses. To get away from enemies, an octopus can squirt **ink**. It does this when it is scared. The ink hides the octopus while it gets away.

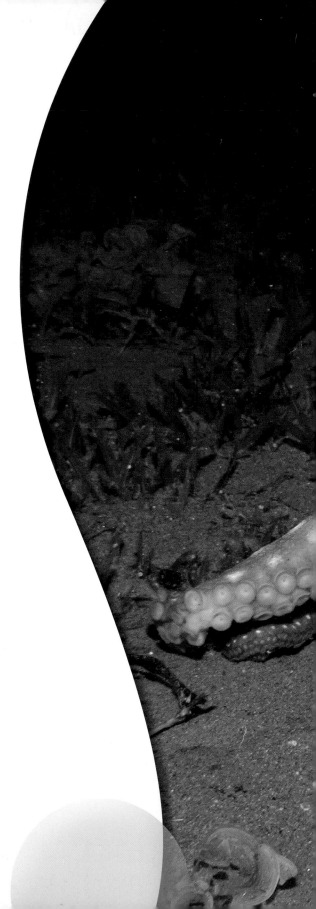

Octopuses are very smart. They can use tools. They are able to learn things. They are important animals in the sea.

Did you know?

Octopuses can live up to 5 years.

GLOSSARY

beak (BEEK): The strong, pointy jaw of an octopus is its beak.

den (DEN): A den is an octopus's home or hiding place.

ink (INK): Ink is a dark, bad-tasting liquid an octopus can squirt from its body. It helps the octopus get away without being seen.

mantle (MAN-tull): A mantle is an octopus's head area.

species (SPEE-sheez): A type of a certain animal. There are about 300 species of octopuses.

TO LEARN MORE

On the Web

Visit our Web page for
lots of links about octopuses:
www.childsworld.com/links

Note to parents, teachers, and librarians:
We routinely verify our Web links to make
sure they are safe, active sites—
so encourage your readers
to check them out!

In the Library

Jackson, Ellen. *Octopuses One to Ten*. San Diego, CA:
Beach Lane Books, 2016.

Macheske, Felicia. *Awesome Arms: Octopus*. Ann Arbor, MI:
Cherry Lake Publishing, 2016.

Shoemaker, Kate. *Octopus Ink*. New York, NY:
Gareth Stevens Publishing, 2015.

INDEX

About the Author

Kara L. Laughlin is an artist and writer who lives in Virginia with her husband, three kids, two guinea pigs, and a dog. She is the author of two dozen nonfiction books for kids.